Pickle was a little kitten.

She had soft brown fur and big green eyes.

Sometimes she was a good little kitten and

sometimes she was not so good.

One day Pickle wanted to play with

her favourite toy.

1

Pickle's favourite toy was a furry grey mouse.
She looked and looked for her favourite toy
but she could not find it.
She looked in the pile of newspapers and
she said,

Pickle's
toys

But the furry grey mouse was not in the
pile of newspapers.

Pickle looked and looked for her favourite toy
but she could not find it.

Then she looked in the basket of wool and
she said,

But the furry grey mouse was not in the
basket of wool.

Pickle looked and looked for her favourite toy
but she could not find it.

Then she looked in the tissue box and
she said,

But the furry grey mouse was not in the tissue box.

'I give up,' said Pickle, and she went to her basket.

There was something under the blanket.

It was the furry grey mouse.

'Here you are,' said Pickle. 'Now we can play.'

Prrr, prrr!